Why I Cannot Take a Lover

Why I Cannot Take a Lover

POEMS

Grace Cavalieri

Washington Writers' Publishing House
Washington, D.C.

COVER DESIGN by Andrew Sargus Klein
TYPOGRAPHY by Barbara Shaw

Library of Congress Control Number: 2022938828
ISBN: 978-1-941551-29-5

WASHINGTON WRITERS' PUBLISHING HOUSE
2814 5th Street, NE, #1301
Washington, D.C. 20017

CONTENTS

FOREWORD

by Caroline Bock

THE DAY I WAS TO MEET GRACE for this interview it was raining, a torrential, flood-warning rain. With this time-bending rain. at nine in the morning, it could be nine at night. I had an hour's drive to Grace's in Annapolis, a home she bought many years ago with her husband, Kenneth Flynn, a noted sculptor, a former Navy pilot, and where she now lives as a widow, alone. I was sure, Grace, a few years older than me, would want to cancel our lunch by the water. She did not. She would, of course, reschedule, if the rain would keep *me* home, but I should not do this because of her. Later that morning, as I pulled into her driveway, Grace greeted me by bounding out to her doorway and waving me in, and I realized that she is one of those people who never get old. I stepped carefully from my mini-SUV and dashed up to her walkway, apologizing for my presumption that she wouldn't want to go out in the rain. I tell her my in-laws are afraid of weather events, afraid to go out even if there was a threat of rain, and she said, "a thought for a poem." I somehow think everything is a thought for a poem for Grace Cavalieri.

This interview took place on schedule at her home and over lunch at a lovely seafood restaurant looking out onto the rain-soaked bay, the tied-up boats, and the docks bucking in the wind. Grace wore her black leather coat and steel-gray, pixie-cut hair. She had a table reserved for us, and I felt like I was in the presence of literary royalty, or just the mother I never had.

I wanted to talk with her about *Why I Cannot Take A Lover,* a slim collection of poems first published by The Washington Writers' Publishing House in 1975 for $2.00 as noted on the inside cover; twenty-six narrative, imagistic poems with a voice and cadence and heart that still resonate today. She didn't have to justify to me why she couldn't take a lover because I was in love already with her, and her poetry. I am an admirer of her literary breadth as a playwright and poet, as a Library of Congress podcaster to the State of Maryland poet laureate, and as a mother and grandmother and master writing teacher. Here is some of what we discussed over a warm grilled salmon salad as droplets pinged against the floor-to-ceiling windows, and outside the wind stirred the water of the bay.

Q: Tell me about *Why I Cannot Take A Lover*...**what inspired these poems?**

A: There's a little melancholy in this book. I wrote this in the late 1960s and early 1970s when I was trying to balance being a wife and mother to four. I was also a Navy wife—for twenty-five years. My spirit was free but my body had to make dinner. I adored my children. But the artist in me was beating against the walls until I started writing. The world was beckoning me. I was first a playwright. In 1966, I had my first play produced, "What Shall We Do Yesterday." Then, I started writing poetry, *this* poetry.

Q: When you look back on these poems now, almost fifty years, what do you think?

A: About the past. The past is where grief is – the past is where so many of the poems are. The reason we write is because we are separated from the past—and we want to exist in it again, for a moment.

Q: What advice do you have for writers trying to balance their lives these days?

A: Take five minutes. Take ten minutes, if you can. Take this time in the morning for yourself. Hold a space for yourself, mentally and physically. If you can do this for ten minutes, you can write anything. I really believe everyone has a story. If you can speak or imagine speech, you can write. When I teach writing, I say give yourself courage. That's the advice I give: Courage, writers.

Q: The literary world focuses much attention on young writers, and I love reading young writers, but what about writers of a certain age, what specific advice do you have for people like me?

A: Like all really alive people, we want to know what we can do next. Poetry is the water for me. It's hydration for me. I'm immersed in poetry every day of my life. I am either reading, writing, broadcasting, or teaching poetry. I am in the flow that is always enriching me. I do think writers fail to take chances—because of a lack of courage, because of fear. My fear? If I read or see bad writing or art, it raunches me out. I think I can never write again. And then I think, how one day, we will be separated from everything we ever loved –so I say, grab on, grab on. Go forward. I've tried to do a book a year or a project a year for the last twenty years. I just clear the deck. The people—especially women—who are artists and writers never grow old. If you create all the time, you are bringing in such energy, such radiation; it's a currency.

Q: In one of the poems, "The Good Life," you reference D.C. as "the poetry capital of the world." Do you still believe that?

A: The writing community here, especially the community of poets, is a tribe. It was back then, and I think it still is. I don't know why the DC-area is different from a New York or San Francisco, but it is. We created a universe and we populated it here. And now the old guard is in the wings, but there is a structure that exists of compassion and comradery.

Q: In another poem, "The Abortion" the narrator is speaking plaintively about the most personal and difficult choices a woman can make. Is this poem about you?

A: Yes. I would have been dead at thirty-five without this operation. Read the line closely, "Says 'Why are you crying?' (name?)." The poem says it all; I don't have to say more, do I?

Q: How would you describe this collection—and the great body of your poetry as a whole?

A: My work is mediative, surreal, coming from a deep pool. It's about holding the space—and time.

Q: You have interviewed so many poets for your past Public Radio program and these days for your current "Poet and the Poem" podcast, I am wondering who is your favorite poet?

A: If poetry is the context for the wound, *no,* poetry is the context of the wound— Louise Glück describes the wound better than anyone I know. All of us writing are just describing the wound, but how do you want to hear it expressed? Louise Glück expresses it better *to me* than anyone else. So minimal. So unadorned. A lack of artifice. It's just primal. It's like a howl. But we resonate with different people. Her wound might not be your wound. I have the only radio recordings of Louise Glück that exist. I've done twenty-five years of interviews without interruption with the Library of Congress and before those twenty years with WPFW-FM. George Washington University Gelman Library Special Collections, which has the "Grace Cavalieri Papers" and archives, is working to digitize all my interviews for prosperity.

Q: Your poems are grounded in relationships, but there's something else within most of them, sometimes an epiphany, more often an aliveness. In your recent collection *Grace Art: Poems and Paintings*, you share your new artistry, vivid abstract painting (Poet's Choice Publishing, 2021). You have a poem in there I keep coming back to, *Tell Me A Story in Any Language* which starts, "Tell me about that 'God,' again..." I feel I can ask you this without irony: Tell me about God.

A: You know that God is the one stream of light that animates everything in this world. The brain and the mind are the animations and the light. It's within us. How else could we possibly do this?

Q: You've started painting, lush abstract paintings. Does painting give you something different than writing?

A: I have to wake up and create. I have to create *anew*, and since the pandemic, it's included painting; it's included poetry. It's about creation.

After our lunch, a mist surrounds us, replenishing, enveloping, a rain of seeds and new growth. When I am home, I ramble through Grace Cavalieri's original chapbook and find myself, in a day of small miracles, at this poem "Hydroplaning":

> Love   It is love   It rains/
> This present is love (and this copy of/
> A present is love) (weather permitting).

The Washington Writers' Publishing House is proud to present this new edition of *Why I Cannot Take a Lover*. This small, nonprofit, cooperative, all-volunteer press would not exist without its co-founder Grace Cavalieri—and her courage, her words, her love.

Caroline Bock
Co-president
The Washington Writers' Publishing House
2022

TALKING HIM IN

I've got the lightest foot
And the heaviest hand
The man on the ledge
Said
I love you   I said
Look
I etch it on your
Exact blood   It's the truth
Like a light which goes on
See
Let me touch you with
Even the slightest of
Left hands
Pentacostal
As a breather beneath water
Where we wake
To the middle day
Together   together
His main vein tied off
From the sun's eyes
Failing   failing
I dreamed his dream
I hold him how to
Cope with poison ivy
I said there are visible implements
The plumbing's good here
I can cook
They make plastic body organs now
There is brightness
Higher than the moon and stars

The scared birds
Chattered to each other
Laying out odds
On their safe air.

HEADLINES

Like the sounds beyond recovery
Like blue
Deep in the stomach
Like a white knife in a room
Glittering
Like a steel lamp
Hard as an element
Real
Dawn
Like the cricket caught sealed
Inside the wall
Singing our good luck.

THE GOOD LIFE

Things are getting simpler—
It's been five years
Since I was alone in the house.
I'm sitting on my bunk having

a candlelight dinner
a library card in bed with me
in Washington, D.C.
The poetry capital of the world.

SIT UP AND TAKE NOTICE

The sign says
"The Ice Capades Is Coming To Town"

Only the naturalists
                    will survive
Be mindful of this
He says, wild flowers

Wild flowers, wild flowers
As soon as you love someone
You give something up
                    (wild)
The note reads

I kiss him twice
(Why send him off
        on just
                one wing?)
A face like a leather doll

                wild flowers,
I whisper

I am too quiet, he says
(Flowers)
Quiet is what people look like
(Wild
Flowers)
That's not what they are.

DON'T UNDERSELL YOURSELF

Consider the brown cow
Eating green grass
Giving white milk

THE ABORTION

The counselors have been trained
To say your name every sentence
Over and over they say your
Name every sentence your name
That's how you know you are a person
That's how you know you are a person
You can hear it
Even if you cry and the doctor
Says "Why are you crying (name)?"
And you tell him and he says
"Name, the world is changing."

After, there is an assortment of
Saltines and cookies.

JANUARY

The grave is untended
I did not see your sound
Gone
Bounced off the house
Across the road
Where I now live

Radios still play
While you sleep
Did you know

Old lovers
Call me Ma'am

At night
I lean into my hand
Flesh microphone
Leaning in
Whispering
Good Night
Good Night
To each of you
The baby I'll never hold
The father in his ground

To each of you
Silence carries
Settles its land

Quiet snow
Falls from my heart
Covering the sky.

FIGHTING OFF THE RESCUE TEAM

For Paz

When the man in the elevator
Reached in his raincoat
               to show you
"Something nice, Honey"
You closed your eyes tight
               but it was only a tux
                and a rose like
Nice old men wore in the movies
Before we were scared
              men sweet enough to melt in the rain

Outside your window
You staring after, your young
Hair on your shoulders.

WHY CAN'T YOU LOVE ME, I SAID

I could never love anyone named whatever
You're named, he answered.

SPEECH TO A WEED
SAYING WHO I LOVE
DOESN'T REQUIRE IT TO BE A FLOWER

Because being rejected is a sin and you
Are the opposite of sin

Which makes you a special substance before burning,
Delicious without being drunk or smoked

I am safe in your shade like a large yellow hat
Or diplomatic immunity

Things spinning for your sake
Like the pearl in my wrist which is my pulse saying

Thank you, thank you
The solitude outside, lonely, changed

To quiet inside where once there were crowds

And appreciation from my fingertip which was
Pressed to that wood door (brown) when it closed

I just wanted to go to that school to know everything
Things other people know and write and say

The train went by with its lamp
I was thrown on my back in the bushes

You woke me up by the pond giving me back
My fantasies, the only pleasure I thought were lost

I know so much about loving you, that's why I cry.

FROM: THE ENTERTAINER

To the children who cry and are not comforted
To the taster who cannot swallow
To those attracting what we hate
To the children who are not comforted
          (People, those running vaulting skipping
Those pogo sticks who fail as persons
                    who do not comfort)

The futility in what you cannot have
The hunting game where all are prey
The children who are not comforted

To the age which shows in my wrists
In wrinkles from waving goodbye
Don't cry children goodbye waving
Waving waving waving.

TOUCH

Last night
We were sitting in a room
One square tall

I wore red
It seemed the proper thing to wear

I had the new baby
I didn't want to go to work

I thought maybe
I could stay at home and
Take of my baby

But in a room so small?
What would I do
In a room so small all day

Outside it is confusing
A city near water
I have created a hundred cities
By the water

Fantastic cities which look like
Amsterdam and Colorado
But never existed before

In which I set out trying
To memorize the way back to the room
Or place or school

In which this particular dream will
Dwell
Like a small floral offering.

SPECIES

In making love to a cat
Action itself is not a virtue

The meow goes right through your heart
But his eyes search out bugs.

Scream, beg, talk in his idiom,
Say things are better than they were before
No.

Shade and milk
And economic enslavement
Determine your value.

This is why trusting animals
Which fall into wrong hands are slaughtered.

And I can see why.

I WON'T DANCE. DON'T ASK ME.

I'm the perfect fantasy
Rented out for weddings barmitzvahs
And other occasions
What I need is someone
To put veins in my arms
Then pump stuff in the veins red as
The metaphor for love.

I wouldn't like to live in any forest
Because if the trees get too dry
It would be a fire because
Lightning makes the biggest fire
But the pictures of forests O Baby
They drip off me like bad fur
And make us all think
We've actually been somewhere near the trees.

THE HAT OVER THE HEART

The replica of the Eiffel tower
Is forbidden to be sold by vendors

This is how it should be
                              souvenirs
Should be prohibited by law

Carloads of pleasures make
Unsuspecting passersby hopeful

The data technology corporation
          is replacing sanscrit

On the ground there is talk of
The sexually assaulted

                    of people
Tired enough to go the speed limit

There has been a failure
At the Library of Congress

From this ballast I go on
              my many excursions
The weight of nostalgia mean nothing

There is snow in the upper air
              elemental
                         I rise

Heat may be better for headaches

        than ice
I hear

From a long way away, a long way away.

VIRTUES

1.

I cannot take your pain but
Neither will I ever dance to the man
Who dies. I know a girl who loved so much
When she mourned the death of a rabbit,
Hair grew out of each her pores.

2.

Cut away the Love to where
The bone stops grieving. Cut blossoms
Off basil, my instructions say,
"Fooling the plant into Summer."

3.

If you love anything too much to cut,
You'll get a dimple on your finger. It'll
Never go away. The finger will not work.

HYDROPLANING

It is raining heavy at times triggering
High way over the roadway

It will rain at times

We will hear this news by radio

Please before eleven o'clock
Open your birthday present

It is the best I could do

Love   It is love   It rains

This present is love (and this copy of
A present is love) (weather permitting)

I AM NOT LAZY. THIS IS ONE THING I AM NOT.

For Ken

I keep a tidy kitchen.
When irreparable damage had been done
I gave up smoking but for maybe just
One cigar day. I emptied all the trays.
When news reached us of the undue
Hardships I divided the wind as
A factor, the speed as a factor
And puffed up the pillows in the next room.
When armies of enemies and friends advanced
Unlimited, I saw someone who looked
Like your wife and bought a
Picture of her for you to put on your desk.
When bullets hit dead center I said
What is the use of all the people we
Did not love and who did not love us.
I put them out with the garbage.
Before we killed an animal for
Supper we begged his pardon on
Our knees like Cherokees.
When strong currents ripped away
The wall I claimed it was the
Only way to stop the runaway cars.
Tasting the air like snakes without
Noses we've crawled along a long time
Finding our direction.
That's why I can honestly say I am
And have always been a good if not excellent
Housekeeper.

THE COLOR OF MY HAIR

Now I know how few differences there are
Between us and
The terrible distance we the wind.

I have been poor before there was money
As far away as what you want
I have been on the streets
I have seen a flower lady with no flowers
A little boy cross his fingers
I have heard about the coming
Of winter, the religious coming from
The flower seller

You laugh with your head on my belly
Sitting under the table to feel the
Difference, the winds, the rain

Damp air affects my hair.
This is where I would like to ride:
In the back of a car behind glass
Like old ladies
Wearing a dark print flowered dress and a cross.

HOT KISSES

I have never been
In Anyone's memory
Someone said
Say why don't you write
That down about me, so

I did   real perfect
The fantasy wedding scene
Thanks   she said
I needed a little poontang.

MOMENTS

Eat a relish sandwich (between two onion thins)
Put on silver earrings (long)
Have a gin
Break water against a rock (elsewhere)
Sleep like a sickness
Throw your soul into the air
(Like crumbs of star)
Burning from pain
Raise flowers (from the sand)
(If you can)
Flop silent (like a fish) upon the shore
(Several times) if anyone approaches
Prevent decay
Taste dew like blood
Wander (adorned)
Remove the arrow from a rabbit's heart
(Open yourself
Catch what falls out)
Suspend belief (to the best of your ability)
In case of friendly monkeys
Have a grape (on hand)
Assess etiquette (for failing)
Or allergies to the moon
Wear a white cross
Keep children (on your eye)
Disbelieve petals (of sun) have no roots
Or that the poor don't have
Clean underwear
Or that I have not planned your escape
(Where we'll lunch in the garden)
Further and higher.

AT THE SIGHT OF THE FLAG

We are not
Origins of thought
But someone
To tell a dream to
Practicing our art
Making it look easy
I cannot
Tap dance
My mouth does not move
When the puppet talks
I have been known
To wear
A green and white stocking cap
To be seen
At midnight
Holding my own hand
As appealing as you are
Sobbing throughout
Are you willing to die for this.

THREE CONSECUTIVE DAYS

Done in by the gentle stick
You still sleep
No smells of ironing to remind you
There was a woman here
Your despair
No poetess could make worse
The feminist decorum is
A burial
Where gross now waves goodbye
Six A M Wednesday
Buy measuring cups, thermometers
New toweling
It is all there on the wall
The paper I made to write on as
I leave
Tired, alone, awake, listing adjectives
Steeled against love, liquor, or frenzy
This is the author's note
Left on the refrig
It says everything has a design
Circles, squares, relationships, mind, soul
I reach outside by way of the back porch
Instinct, passion, power, violence
Peas, carrots, jello
So much emptiness the wind blows and
I say Who Is It?

LOOKING MORE LIKE OURSELVES THAN EVER

We walk
One foot higher than the other
As if on a curb
Through the field

But we are not terrified.
Cooks gather
This time of day, in kitchens

Returning juices to the meat
Making preparations through shaded doors

It is possible to be grateful here.

Children play about the house
And other growing things
Commemoration occurs

It is the reason we go inside.

WHY I CANNOT TAKE A LOVER

In the middle of the day
I awake to find the same place
Outside as
When I was ten I
Wished to know again the yards of
Bridal wreath and maple trees side by side
Down to the end of the tracks that bend the
Gypsy's shack where horses were
Unkempt I said Please Let Me Find This Way
As it was when
Rows of trees outside the way back home
Downstairs the woman I am now was
Entertaining ladies laughing talking
Children coming home from school I
Dreamed of tea and wished to rise a child
Begging to find that it was true in
Two levels of this house the dream went on
Elaine my friend would she come no
It is gone it is gone downstairs the woman in me
Entertained the voices in the dream I
Must never sleep within the middle
Of the day in twenty years or more I will wake
To wake again to wish outside for
This hill below our own the school
Nearby the pavement white for walking but
It will not be so no
Matter where we are it will not
Be so the leaf against the window frozen on
Its stalk by changes in the weather I
Wake in time for dinner I
Cooked lima beans the fish
Is fried tomatoes stewed there is rice

Made in hot broth
I wake up to prepare a supper
Sitting by the stove for warmth

THIS IS A TRUE STORY

Watching the children from a distance
The clear blue eye of the horse
Dreams
What he sees rides him
Seated between his large muscles
Like rocks   on top
Sways a man
Dreaming a horse
See him
On the highway   I walk by
Dress pinned up
Dust is kicked from what is tied to the post

Photo by Michael Morgan, 2022

GRACE CAVALIERI, Maryland's tenth Poet Laureate, is author of 26 books and chapbooks of poetry and several short-form and full-length plays. Her new poetry books   are *The Secret Letters of Madame de Stael* (Goss183, 2021;) *Grace Art-Poems and Paintings* (Poets' Choice, 2021;) *What The Psychic Said,* (Goss 183, 2019;) and *Showboat,* (Goss183, 2018) about 25 years as a Navy wife. Her latest play "Quilting The Sun" was produced at the Theater for the New City, NYC in 2019. She founded and still produces "The Poet and The Poem" for public radio, now from the Library of Congress, celebrating 45 years on-air. Grace holds The A.W.P's George Garrett Award, the Pen-Syndicated-Fiction, the Allen Ginsberg, Bordighera Poetry, and Paterson Poetry awards; The Folger Shakespeare Library Columbia Award; and The CPB Silver Medal. Forthcoming (from The Word Works '22) is "The Long Game: New and Selected Poems."

CAROLINE BOCK is the author of *Carry Her Home*, winner of the Fiction Award from the Washington Writers' Publishing House, and *LIE* and *Before My Eyes,* young adult novels, from St. Martin's Press. The winner of the 2018 *Writer* magazine story award and the 2021 Adrift story award from Driftwood Press, she is also the fiction editor of the anthology *This Is What America Looks Like: poetry and fiction from DC, Maryland, and Virginia* and co-editor of the literary journal *WWPH Writes.* Her creative work has appeared in *SmokeLong, Ploughshares, Brevity, Gargoyle, the Grace & Gravity series* and more. She has been honored with an Artists & Scholars Award from Montgomery County Arts & Humanities Council in Maryland. In 2011, she earned an MFA in Fiction from The City College of New York. In 2022, she became co-president with the poet Jona Colson of the Washington Writers' Publishing House.

More from the Washington Writers' Publishing House

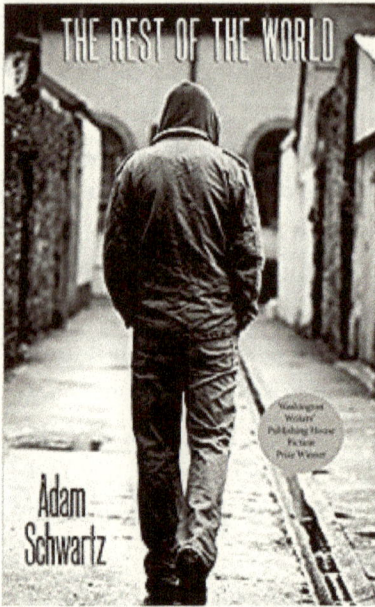

THE REST OF THE WORLD

Adam Schwartz

2020 Fiction Award-winner

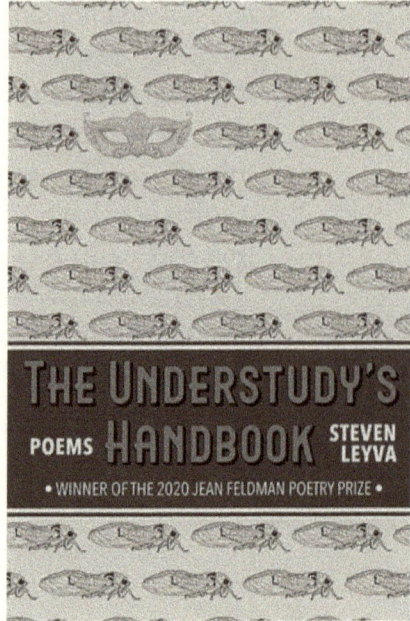

THE UNDERSTUDY'S HANDBOOK

POEMS   STEVEN LEYVA

• WINNER OF THE 2020 JEAN FELDMAN POETRY PRIZE •

**2020
Jean Feldman
Poetry Award**

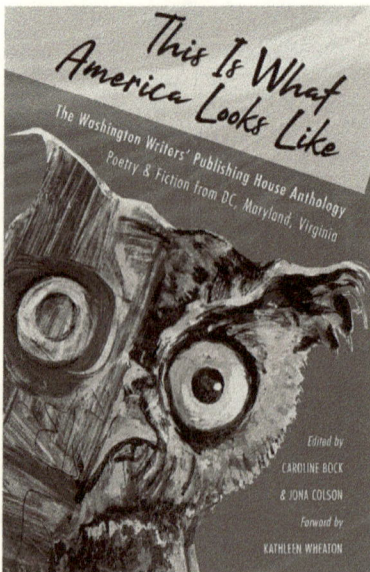

*This Is What
America Looks Like*

The Washington Writers' Publishing House Anthology

Poetry & Fiction from DC, Maryland, Virginia

Edited by
CAROLINE BOCK
& JONA COLSON

Forward by
KATHLEEN WHEATON

**111 works of
short fiction and poetry
by 100 writers on the
creative state of America**

More WWPH books here:

WWPH is an independent, nonprofit, cooperative press founded in 1975. Our mission is to publish and celebrate writers from DC, Maryland, and Virginia. To learn more about our fiction, poetry, and creative nonfiction manuscript contests, our bi-weekly literary journal, and to purchase more WWPH books, please visit:

www.washingtonwriters.org

Follow us on:
Twitter@wwphpress
Facebook@WWPH
Instagram@writingfromWWPH

Contact us at:
wwphpress@gmail.com

PROUD MEMBER

COMMUNITY OF LITERARY MAGAZINES & PRESSES
W W W . C L M P . O R G

WWPH is a proud recipient of a
Creativity Grant from

DEPARTMENT OF COMMERCE maryland state arts council